Karen &

Parenting Us

How God Does It

Includes the text of Scripture passages studied

12 studies for neighborhood,
student, and church groups

Harold Shaw Publishers
Wheaton, Illinois

All Scripture quotations in this publication are from *The Holy Bible: New International Version.* Copyright © 1973, 1978, 1984 by International Bible Society. Used by permission of Zondervan Bible Publishers.

ISBN 0–87788–669–5

Cover photo: Carlos Vergara

Library of Congress Cataloging-in-Publication Data

Mains, David R.
  Parenting us.

  1. God—Fatherhood. 2. Children of God.
3. Christian life—1960- . I. Mains, Karen
Burton. II. Title.
BT153.F3M3 1986   231.7   86-6620
ISBN 0–87788–669–5

95   94   93   92   91   90   89   88   87

10   9   8   7   6   5   4   3   2

CONTENTS

Letter to Group Members   5
Notes to Group Leaders   9
Study 1/Daddy, Do You Love Me?   13
Study 2/Who Am I?   19
Study 3/Our Heavenly Parent's
          Two Great Expectations   27
Study 4/An In-Depth Relationship with God   33
Study 5/You Look Like Your Dad   42
Study 6/Spiritual Sibling Squabbles   47
Study 7/Pulling Your Own Weight   53
Study 8/Who Do You Love the Most?   60
Study 9/How Shall We Behave?   66
Study 10/New Beginnings   73
Study 11/Reading of the Greatest Will   80
Study 12/Being Children Again   86
Weekly Leader's Notes   92

LETTER TO GROUP MEMBERS

Thoughts on being parented by God

When my mother died two years after my father, I was amazed by how orphaned I felt—I, a middle-aged adult, with children of my own. How lonely I was in the exploration of this new human vacuum; there was no one who had known me ever since I had been an infant, no one to call to ask for the ingredients for a special family recipe. *There was no one who would listen to me with my father's profound and concentrated attention.*

After my mother's funeral, I was standing in our walk-in closet, getting dressed; but mostly, I was complaining to the Lord. "If I knew my children were hurting," I said, "I would try to ease their pain, and if my parents were here and knew I was hurting, they would reach out to me in some way."

Putting on a jacket I hadn't worn for a season, I continued with my diatribe. "I need you to be my parent, but the problem is: I don't know if I can trust you to be the kind of parent I need you to be!"

Thrusting my hand into the pocket of the jacket, I discovered three forgotten dollar bills—not a lot of money in terms of our modern economy.

"This is not what I had in mind—" I began, but my protest was interrupted by the sudden, clear inner word, *Karen, Karen, if you allow yourself to have a child's emotional needs, you will only receive a child's allowance.*

And at that moment I relaxed because I recognized this as excellent parenting. Grief after loss is healthy and necessary in the seesaw process of restoring emotional balance, but self-pity—self-pity—is an inward negative fixation that prohibits psychological progress.

I was no longer an orphan, and I knew it. God was parenting me.

How often after my parents' death, people confided that they, too, had lost a parent. Invariably, they would say something to this effect: "I miss my parents more now than I did when they died."

The truth is, no matter how old we become, we always need to be parented. We need someone more mature than ourselves. We need someone who has a longer, clearer perspective on life. We need someone who cares for us in a good parent's particular, special way.

God is that One who always parents us, who is wiser, who is in a generation beyond our own, who has the eternal perspective on life. In fact, he is our true Parent. The adoptive or biological parents we have known during our earthly sojourn are only his surrogates.

Unfortunately, there are many who are emotionally or psychologically deformed because of the inadequacy of earthly parenting. They have deprivations so deep that only the love of their Parent, God, can fill the bottomless pit. Years of counseling have taught me that hope for these people is discovered when they make connection with the active, lavish love of the heavenly Father.

But we all need that heavenly Parent—this has been my surprising, recent discovery.

Each one of us must experience a childlike dependency transference if we are to achieve spiritual maturity. We must learn to detach our child-trust from our human mom and dad and attach it to the One who can be both mother and father to us eternally.

Great is thy faithfulness,
O God my Father,
There is no shadow of turning with thee;
Thou changest not, thy compassions, they fail not;
As thou hast been thou forever wilt be.

This book is more than just a Bible studyguide. Here you will find exercises that assist you to see that God considers himself to be your true Parent and that he has recorded his parenting intents in Scripture. But, even more important, we want to help you to *experience* that truth. David and I will remain unsatisfied if you simply discover how frequently this theme is reiterated in the Bible. Our goal is for you to integrate the truth of God's Fatherhood in your life. Only then will you be on your way to understanding and applying *Parenting Us: How God Does It.*

Karen Mains

NOTES TO GROUP LEADERS

How do you start your group?

A desire for spiritual growth both for oneself and for others forms the basis for establishing a worthwhile Bible study. Don't set your hopes on huge numbers. God's Holy Spirit will bring those to the group that he chooses. Where to begin? Invite those whose names the Spirit whispers in your mind and heart as you pray about getting this study started.

Size? Time? Period of study?

A good size for a group is two to eight people. When the group reaches ten to twelve, some disadvantages appear—such as fewer feeling free to participate. Groups that grow too big can offset such a problem by dividing into two smaller groups for discussion.

A group needs to meet regularly enough to encourage good communication. Once a week or every two weeks is good—once a month makes it difficult to keep continuity. Establish a time period (goal) for completing the study, such as twelve or twenty-four weeks. Group members will be motivated to commit themselves to regular attendance when they are able to see a time frame. At least two hours per session will allow for in-depth discussion and fulfilling satisfactory interaction with the Word.

Whose group is this anyway?

Group members—working, studying, praying together—make up the group. A leader's primary function is to facilitate discussion. Some groups prefer to pass this responsibility around rather than choose just one person; for many studies that is an effectual kind of leadership. For these studies the leader should probably be the person with the best group skills.

Parenting Us: How God Does It is unique. In a sense it is quite different from other inductive Bible studies because three of the exercises, TEST YOURSELF, DEBRIEF AS A GROUP, and LISTEN TO YOUR HEAVENLY PARENT, are designed to impact life experience with conceptual truth, which we receive imaginatively and emotionally as well as cerebrally. These exercises gently integrate the meanings of Scripture. Approaching this study's topic with merely intellectual objectivity would be frustrating because of the way in which the study is designed.

This Bible study is not primarily designed to help you learn how to be a better parent but to help you learn how to be parented by God. While a side effect of experiencing this major truth may well be the development of parenting skills for those who are in active parenting roles, the major goal of this study is for group members to experience that they are children of a heavenly Father.

The topic of being parented by God is a profound truth which evokes deep psychological and emotional responses. In order for us to understand how God parents us, we need to examine the bedrock of our lives—that primary relationship between ourselves and our own parents. The way we relate or have related to our parents influences our adult emotional and psychological maturity; it is also crucial in determining the way we perceive God the Father, and how we relate to him.

This study has life-changing potential. Enormous healing strength is available to the Christian who not only understands that God is the heavenly Parent but who begins to live and act in the center of that truth.

The group leader of this study must exercise gifts of sensitivity, insight, and compassion. You are likely to have adults in your group who have recently lost their parents (or who are subconsciously grieving over the loss of a parent in childhood). You may have people with a neglectful, abusive past. You may have grown-ups still suffering from the effects of their own parents' divorce.

The goal of these studies is to present from Scripture the truth that God, our heavenly Parent, is superior to any earthly parent, and then to help individual members make the emotional and spiritual transference based on this truth that will free them for a divine-human relationship that will last through eternity.

The Holy Spirit, working through you, sensitizing you and filling you with his loving compassion, can do exactly this in the weeks ahead.

Read through the following *Ideas For Group Leaders*. Then review the *Weekly Leader's Notes* which begin on page 92. These give you a brief overview, the key emphasis, the response desired, and any additional ideas that seem pertinent for each week. The group leader's preparation should begin with prayer, an examination of the *Weekly Leader's Notes* for the appropriate week, and time to become familiar with the workbook material, including the Scripture passage.

You may use the optional sections of the study that make use of cassettes—11-minute recordings of broadcasts of The Chapel of the Air—the form in which David and Karen Mains originally presented this material. Although the study stands on its own, we recommend

that you avail yourself of this resource as well. The cassette material takes much of the responsibility for group interaction off the
shoulders of the leader, adds variety and a positive dynamic to the
study time, and stimulates additional ideas in regard to the Scripture that is being studied.

Pointers for Leaders

1/Allow time for group members to think through the questions.
Don't be afraid of silence; often it is an indication that people are
thinking, so allow them that privilege. In fact, silence is so important to the growth process that one section of the weekly group
time, LISTEN TO YOUR HEAVENLY PARENT, is deliberately
planned to provide beneficial quiet.

2/Encourage a diversity of answers, and much participation in the
discussion of each question. If there is a lag, you can ask, "What do
the rest of you think?" or "How do you feel about this, John?"
Often shy members will respond to this personal nudging. Be sure
to avoid the temptation to answer the questions for the group.
Allow them to think and come to conclusions for themselves.

3/To stimulate discussion, activate the group's thinking with comments such as—"Would you explain that further?" "Can you give a
specific example?" "Show us in the text where you found that idea."

4/Avoid tangents. If you see the discussion veering off-course,
tactfully point out the main issue under discussion once again.

5/As leader, try to strike a balance yourself between contributing
too much and too little. Over-talking can stifle others; on the other
hand, don't leave the group directionless.

6/Controversy can sometimes threaten people; but it doesn't need
to! Differences of opinion can stimulate ideas, even if the issue is
not completely resolved. Agree to disagree agreeably.

7/Each broadcast (except broadcasts 6 and 11) ends with tips for
parents, practical ideas parents can apply to their own children. The
cassette cue line instructs you to turn off the cassette before each
tip and instructions in each study will also give you this tip. As a
group leader you can decide (depending on the nature of your
group—do they have children? Are they single? Are they interested?
Is there time?) to play the rest of the cassette, or to discuss the idea.

1

Daddy, Do You Love Me?

Christians, regardless of age, need to experience
the security of God's parental love.

*H*OW FREQUENTLY LITTLE CHILDREN ASK, "Daddy—Mommy—do
you love me?" The ease with which we understand, accept, and
experience our heavenly Parent's love is often determined by the
quality of love we experienced in our childhood. Just as every child
needs to know he is loved, every Christian (child of the heavenly
Parent), regardless of age, needs to experience the security of God's
love.

Test Yourself

Take the following self-evaluation test. It will help you participate
better in the group discussion.

In question one, circle the answer that best relates to your own
upbringing. In questions two through four, circle the correct word
and place an "F" for father, and "M" for mother (or "FM" for both)
next to the appropriate phrases.

1/I was certain of the love of my:
a/mother
b/father
c/both parents
d/neither parent
e/grandparents

2/My parents expressed their love:
a/verbally
b/physically
c/with material gifts
d/not at all

3/As a child, I heard the words, "I love you,"
a/frequently
b/every so often
c/rarely
d/never that I can remember

4/My knowledge that my parents loved me was:
a/on a deep emotional level.
b/only in my head.
c/I was never sure—sometimes I thought they did; sometimes I was afraid they didn't.
d/lacking; for some reason, my parents were unable to love me.

5/Choose a few adjectives that describe the love that existed in your family:

_____

_____

_____

6/I recognize God's love for me in the following ways:
a/through reading Scripture.
b/during Sunday morning worship.
c/when I am with other Christians.

d/through answered prayers.
e/in private moments of devotion.
f/through evidence of his care for me.
g/in my family relationships.
h/as I function on the job.
i/other _____

7/I know God loves me in my head; on the emotional level I feel his love:
a/at most moments of my life.
b/when everything is going well.
c/only during crises.
d/every once in a while.
e/rarely.
f/I have trouble experiencing God's love.

8/Choose a few adjectives to describe your heavenly Parent's love:

_____

_____

Play Audio Cassette (Optional)

(Leaders: *Cue cassette (Parenting Us: How God Does It)* to Day One, "Daddy, Do You Love Me?"

Stop cassette just after Karen Mains says, "I don't think they will ever heal from those deprivations until they experience the love of God, the Parent.")

Debrief as a Group

1/Share with the group the words you chose to describe the love you experienced in your family and explain briefly why you chose those words.

2/What words did you use to describe God's love? Did you choose these words because you know that they are true? Have you experienced them to be true?

3/Is there a correlation between the love you received from your parents and the kind of love you are experiencing from God?

Scripture Search

Yet, O Lord, you are our Father; We are the clay, you are the potter; we are all the work of your hand (Isa. 64:8).

Do not be like them, for your Father knows what you need before you ask him. This, then, is how you should pray: Our Father in heaven . . . (Matt. 6:8–9a).

Can a mother forget the baby at her breast and have no compassion on the child she has borne? Though she may forget, I will not forget you! (Isa. 49:15).

I will not leave you as orphans; I will come to you (John 14:18).

The Lord appeared to us in the past, saying: I have loved you with an everlasting love; I have drawn you with loving-kindness (Jer. 31:3).

In the LEFT-hand column, choose a phrase for each verse above that shows the kind of relationship God has with us. Share these with the group.

God is: I have a Heavenly Parent who:

1/   **1**/

2/   **2**/

3/   **3**/

4/   **4**/

5/   **5**/

Then, in the RIGHT-hand column, write a personal response to the phrases listed on the first side beginning with the words, "I have a heavenly Parent who . . ."

Pretend that you are a child who has just asked, "Daddy, do you love me?" Look at the Scriptures again. Write down a summary sentence that indicates what God's response might be:
My dear child,

_____

_____

_____

More Group Work

Think about one time when you experienced God as your heavenly Parent. Now, share these experiences with each other.

Listen to Your Heavenly Parent

In your heart pray, "Father, do you love me?" Now write out Jeremiah 31:3, but substitute your own name for the pronoun "you."

_____

_____

_____

Tips to Parents (Optional)

(Leaders: *Begin the cassette* at the previous stop to hear the final segment on tips for parents.)

1/Realize your children's need for verbalization of your love for them.

2/Note the example of the Jewish Sabbath:
The father affirms each child for a specific action or personality trait
that he approves, and gives each child a kiss or evidence of affec-
tion.

3/Parents who experience God's love will be more able to communicate love to their children.

2

Who Am I?

Self-identity is discovered only in knowing the wonder of
our heavenly parentage.

WHO AM I? This has been the cry of the human heart since the
age of man began. Much of the answer to this question lies in some
form of genealogy research. We understand more of who we are by
understanding where we have come from, who our ancestors were,
the nature and personality of our own parents, and the kind of
family life they achieved.

Test Yourself

Before examining the nature of God's parenting, it will be helpful to
recall some details about your own parents. Begin with the following two self-testing exercises.

How well do I know my parents?

1/My mother's favorite color

_____

2/My father proposed to my mother

_____

3/My father always wanted to

_____

4/Mother's favorite food

_____

5/One of father's strongest values

_____

6/Mother considered that she failed

_____

7/The best time in my father's life

_____

8/My parents became Christians

_____

9/Most of all my mother loved to

_____

10/Mother's favorite relative

11/Mother felt the most important thing she could teach me

12/My father relaxed

13/My father's father's name was

14/Mother dreaded

15/My parents always wanted to travel to

How well do you know your parents? (circle one.)
very well   well   somewhat   not at all

Sometimes the people who are the most influential in our lives are the ones we know the least about. If you know your parents well, why?

If you don't know your parents well, what are the reasons?

If your parents are still alive and in touch with you, consider if any of the Test Yourself questions would be good conversation openers.

"Spitting Image"

Most of us like to think that "we are a combination of the best qualities of both of our parents." This is a remarkable form of self-delusion and it is rarely true! Fill in the following blanks:

1/One positive quality I inherited from my mother

_____

2/One negative quality I inherited from my mother

_____

3/One positive quality I inherited from my father

_____

4/One negative quality I inherited from my father

_____

Debrief as a Group

Take time to remember one pleasant childhood experience that involved either one or both of your parents. Jot down a few details in the space below. Be prepared to share your memory with the group.

_____

_____

Share with each other the pleasant childhood experience you remembered and explain why this memory is still so positive.

Play the Audio Cassette (Optional)

(Leaders: *Cue cassette* to Day Two, "Who Am I?"

Stop cassette just after Karen Mains says, "And I think that we need to understand that he feels for that creation much more than even the human parent—that seems impossible to us who are parents—but he does because of his knowledge and his knowing of that creation.")

Scripture Search

Just as in a human sense we know better who we are when we more fully understand our parentage, so in the spiritual sense we clarify our spiritual identity when we understand our heavenly parentage.

The following companion passages were both written by Paul, and both have been reprinted from his letter to the Ephesians. Both passages refer to the heavenly Father; both passages emphasize the verb *to know,* or synonyms of that verb.

The writer desires that his readers know seven things. The first two have been numbered. Underline the remaining five, number them, then as a group paraphrase each thing the apostle Paul wants his readers to know. Write the suggested paraphrases in the space following the Scripture quotations.

I have not stopped giving thanks for you, remembering you in my prayers. I keep asking that the God of our Lord Jesus Christ, the glorious Father, may give you a spirit of wisdom and revelation, so that (1) you may know him better. I pray also that the eyes of your heart may be enlightened in order that (2) you may know the hope to which he has called you, *the riches of his glorious inheritance in the saints, and his incomparably great power for us who believe . . .* (Eph. 1:16–19).

For this reason I kneel before the Father, from whom his whole family in heaven and on earth derives its name. I pray that out of his glorious riches he may strengthen you with power through his Spirit in your inner being, so that Christ may dwell in your hearts through faith. And I pray that you, being rooted and established in love, may have power together with all the saints, to grasp how wide and long and high and deep is the love of Christ, and to know this love that surpasses knowledge—that you may be filled to the measure of all the fulness of God (Eph. 3:14–19).

Paraphrases:

1/(Example) to know God, to understand him, to know him in an intimate way. . .

2/(Example) the confident assurance . . .

3/ _____

4/ _____

5/ _____

6/ _____

7/ _____

If you were to take a test, *How Well Do You Know Your Heavenly Parent?*, what qualities about the personality of God could you pick out from these two passages? List the group's ideas below:

_____

_____

_____

_____

Listen in the Quiet

Ask yourself: Have I experienced, in any kind of tangible way, these personal qualities of my heavenly Parent? Think about the qualities which the group has just suggested. Choose one quality of God you

experience _____

and one you don't _____

Now define your true feelings about God as your heavenly Parent. Listen closely to the honest, inward murmurings. Write some of those feelings in the following space.

_____

_____

_____

_____

_____

Ask the Holy Spirit to begin revealing these true feelings to you, then silently pray the following prayer:

Dear heavenly Parent,
I need not only the intellectual knowledge that you are truly my Father, but I need to experience the reality of that truth on a

daily level in my life. Help me to learn in these weeks ahead to confidently call you "Daddy." Help me to develop a surprising intimacy with you as my true parent. Help me to *know you* so that I can truly *know who I am*. Help me to find my self-identity in you.
Amen.

Now listen as your study leader reads the words of this same prayer aloud.

Tips for Parents (Optional)

(Leaders: *Begin the cassette* at the previous stop to hear the final segment on tips for parents.)

1/Family is extremely important.

2/As parents we must introduce our family members to their true parent, God, and help them to begin to know who he is.

3

Our Heavenly Parent's Two Great Expectations

God's children function best as they obey his clear
parental guidelines.

*W*HEN WE STUDY ANY PART of God's nature, such as his parental
nature, the Holy Spirit uses our focused attention to teach how the
truth relates to our lives on a daily level. Are there any recent
incidents regarding God's parenting that you want to share with the
group? Has God's parenting ever taken a humorous turn? Do you
have any new insights regarding your personal relationship to your
heavenly Parent?

Scripture Search

Read the following Scripture portion and pretend this is Act I from
the script of a drama to be performed on stage. Imagination may
stimulate some fresh insights into this familiar passage.

*One of them, an expert in the law, tested him with this question:
"Teacher, which is the greatest commandment in the Law?" Jesus
replied: "Love the Lord your God with all your heart and with all
your soul and with all your mind." This is the first and greatest*

commandment. And the second is like it: "Love your neighbor as yourself." All the Law and the Prophets hang on these two commandments (Matt. 22:35–40).

The title of this play is *Two Great Expectations.* Describe:

The setting

The protagonist (main character)

The antagonist (principle opponent)

The dramatic tension (reason for confrontation)

Matthew 22:15 begins with this: "Then the Pharisees went out and laid plans to trap him in his words." Discuss the following questions:

1/How did the Pharisees expect to trap Christ with this lawyer's questions?

2/If you were the director of this drama, how would you instruct the lawyer/actor to interpret his part (tone of voice, body language, etc.)?

3/What do you think Christ's attitude was during this confrontation?

4/How do you think the lawyer and his friends responded to Christ's answer?

The title of this drama, *Two Great Expectations,* is based on Christ's answer. List those two expectations as revealed in the dramatic exchange.

1/ _____

2/ _____

Now pretend that a new book has just appeared on the *New York Times* bestseller list. Read the following excerpt:

If anyone says, "I love God," yet hates his brother, he is a liar. For anyone who does not love his brother, whom he has seen, cannot love God, whom he has not seen. And he has given us this command: Whoever loves God must also love his brother (1 John 4:20).

Everyone who believes that Jesus is the Christ is born of God, and everyone who loves the father loves his child as well. This is how we know that we love the children of God: by loving God and carrying out his commands. This is love for God: to obey his commands. And his commands are not burdensome . . . (1 John 5:1–3).

Describe the following:

The author

_____

The genre (type) of book *(Example: Love manual)*

_____

The theme of the book *(Example: How to learn to love in two difficult lessons)*

_____

Why do you think so many people are buying the book? *(Example: Already a best-selling author)*

_____

_____

In the space below, make a list from both the Matthew and John passages:

Whom we are supposed to love	How we are supposed to love

Both of these passages speak about commandments to love God and our neighbor. Examine each again and think of words that describe to us the *importance* of each of these commandments.

_____

Play the Audio Cassette (Optional)

(Leaders: *Cue cassette* to Day Three, "Two Great Expectations."

Stop cassette just after David Mains says, "God's children function best as they obey his clear parental guidelines . . . I'll say it again, and then I'd like to see if we can give a suggestion to parents who are listening.")

Debrief as a Group

As a group, brainstorm what society would look like if everyone fulfilled Jesus' two great expectations. Start by answering the question: What would this world need less of?

_____

_____

_____

_____

Listen in the Quiet

Pray the following prayer:

> Father,
> I say I love you,
> But I find that I love you not very well,
> And your other children most inadequately.
> Reveal to me in this quiet
> Whom it is I don't love,
> And how I can love you better.

Now listen, then write the initials of one or two people who are hard to love.

_____

Continue the prayer:

> I confess my need to be more like you in my love toward others. Help me to see those I have listed above through your eyes. Show me the beauty you see in each of them.

Take a moment to write some of the qualities of these hard-to-love people that God sees as beautiful.

_____

_____

_____

Remain in prayerful silence and think of two things you can do to better fulfill your heavenly Parent's two great expectations. What one concrete and specific action can you take that will improve your relationship with your hard-to-love people? Write your idea in the following spaces.

_____

_____

_____

What is another specific and measurable goal you can set that will enhance your love toward God? Write this below as a reminder and a promise to yourself.

_____

_____

End with the following prayer:

> My father,
> I will try to do better in fulfilling your two great expectations, but as I struggle to grow in these areas I also need to receive evidences of your parental approval. I need to know that you love me in spite of all my inadequacies.

Tips for Parents (Optional)

(Leaders: *Begin the cassette* at previous stop to hear the final segment for parents.)

1/Children function best when given clear guidelines.

2/Teach them about God's two great expectations. They are easy enough for children to understand and follow.

4

An In-Depth Relationship with God

God's children experience an in-depth relationship when they take advantage of their heavenly Father's intimate communication.

*I*N A HIGHLY TECHNOLOGICAL SOCIETY, where machines and impersonal systems dominate much of our lives, we find ourselves longing for the intimate, interpersonal relationships that make our days meaningful. However, many people have difficulty understanding intimacy; some are even afraid of it. Webster's Dictionary defines intimacy as follows:

> *in·ti·ma·cy,* n. 1. the state or act of being intimate; intimate association; familiarity.

Actually, Webster's isn't very helpful in defining this often-used word. See if the study group can do better.

Debrief as a Group

Define the word *intimacy* by using the word association technique. Answer this question: What other words do you think of when you hear the word intimacy? List the group's ideas below:

_____

_____

_____

_____

Scripture Search

Scripture is, among other things, a record of God's in-depth, or intimate, communication with man. Take a few minutes to think of the names of some biblical characters with whom God seemed to communicate in a deep sort of way. List them here.

_____

_____

_____

Look at Psalm 139:13–18:

For you created my inmost being;
  you knit me together in my mother's womb.
I praise you because I am fearfully and wonderfully made;
  your works are wonderful,
  I know that full well.
My frame was not hidden from you
  when I was made in the secret place.
When I was woven together in the
  depths of the earth,
  your eyes saw my unformed body.

All the days ordained for me
were written in your book
before one of them came to be.
How precious to me are your thoughts,
O God!
How vast is the sum of them!
Were I to count them
they would outnumber the grains of sand.
When I awake,
I am still with you.

As a group, suggest the kinds of intimate knowledge God has of the unborn child. Write the ideas below:

Example: It was God who performed the original ultrasonography!

_____

_____

_____

_____

(Note: Ultrasonography sonogram is the diagnostic use of ultrasonic waves to visualize internal bodily structures and organs.)

Do you remember when you learned that God was omnipresent—present everywhere; and that he was also omniscient—all-knowing? You could not hide from him, and he knew everything about you? If you ever felt this was a terrible truth, try to get in touch with why you had that moment of dread.

_____

_____

Answer the following questions on your own.

1/What is the Psalmist's feeling about this truth as he pens it in this portion of Scripture?

2/What is wonderful about the fact that God knows us so intimately?

3/List the people with whom you have established intimate relationships.

4/Now ask yourself why—what is it in the other person's personality or in your own that allows for you to have this particularly close communication?

More Group Work

As a group, discuss together your answers to question 4. Then consider the following statement: One can only have intimate communication with people who are peers, those who share common interests and who are on your own level. Do you agree or disagree?

Now look at the following verses taken from the Psalms. List the qualities these verses reveal about God that make it possible to have an intimate relationship with him.

The Lord is near to all who call on him, to all who call on him in truth. He fulfills the desires of those who fear him; he hears their cry and saves them (Ps. 145:18–19).

I will instruct you and teach you in the way you should go; I will counsel you and watch over you (Ps. 32:8).

Since my youth, O God, you have taught me, and to this day I declare your marvelous deeds (Ps. 71:17).

I cry aloud to the Lord; I lift up my voice to the Lord for mercy. I pour out my complaint before him; before him I tell my trouble. When my spirit grows faint within me, it is you who know my way. In the path where I walk men have hidden a snare for me (Ps. 142:1–3).

In God, whose word I praise, in the Lord, whose word I praise— in God I trust; I will not be afraid. What can man do to me? (Ps. 56:10–11).

As a father has compassion on his children, so the Lord has compassion on those who fear him; for he knows how we are formed, he remembers that we are dust. As for man, his days are like grass, he flourishes like a flower of the field . . . (Ps. 103: 13–15).

Test Yourself

Finish the following sentence completion test.

1/I am happiest when _____ .

2/Mother was kindest to me _____ .

3/My father never _____ .

4/I like people best _____ .

5/God seems _____ .

6/I was angriest at my parents _____ .

7/When my father and I talked, we _____ .

8/When my father disciplined me, he _____.

9/Prayer is _____.

10/I felt closest to my parents _____.

11/When I am depressed, God _____.

12/My mother should have _____.

13/I always wanted my father to _____.

14/I feel I am losing control when _____.

15/When God disciplines me _____.

16/One thing my parents always said to me was _____

_____.

17/My mother _____.

18/Taking orders _____.

19/One word to describe myself is _____.

20/I know I am loved when _____.

21/I pleased my father _____.

22/One word to describe my mother is _____.

23/I have always wanted _____.

24/God's love _____.

In his book *Help! I'm a Parent!* Bruce Narramore makes this point:

The quality of family life experienced by children affects much more than their emotional adjustment. It seriously influences their spiritual development. A child's image of God is strongly influenced by his relationships with his parents. Since God is an immaterial Person, he is hard for a child to comprehend. Foreseeing this problem, God created a family structure to teach us about his nature.

Look back over the test you have just taken. See if you can make any connections between positive ways your parents modeled who God is. Then see if there are any negative associations you have assumed regarding God because of some unhealthy patterns in your family. Have any of your communication patterns with your heavenly Parent been disrupted because of less-than-healthy communication patterns in your own family?

Play the Audio Cassette (Optional)

(Leaders: *Cue cassette* to Day Four of *Parenting Us: How God Does It,* "An In-Depth Relationship with God."

Stop cassette just after David Mains says, ". . . that is a very big help to me as opposed to just immediately jumping into the praying words.")

Now answer these questions:

1/Have I experienced an in-depth communication with my heavenly Parent?

_____

2/What made intimacy with him possible?

_____

3/What things have prevented intimacy between my heavenly Parent and me, his child?

_____

4/I can describe the pattern of the spiritual intimacy between myself and my heavenly Parent as:

_____

_____

5/What one thing do I know about God's personality from these Scriptures that should change my poor communication to better communication?

_____

_____

Listen to Your Heavenly Parent

Close your eyes and listen as your study leader reads the following paragraphs:

Think of the loveliest spot you have ever visited. (Pause and give time for the group to think of a place.) Maybe it was an arboretum under the care of professional landscapers and gardeners. Maybe it was a waterfall you unexpectedly discovered while following a mountain stream uphill. Perhaps it was miles and miles of prairie, untouched by barbed wire fencing or farmhouses, where the wind bent the long grass in the same direction.

Whatever place this might be, think of it now and think of yourself being there alone without any other person. Yet, in another sense, you know you are not alone. You sense beside you the strong yet gentle presence of the Creator of this beautiful place. You know it to be the presence of God. You think of how he walked with Adam and Eve in the unspoiled place, Eden, of how he talked with them in the cool of the evening. You think that perhaps he asked them,

"How was your day?" You wish that he would talk to you in the same way.

You discover a longing in your own soul for this One, who has said that he is your true heavenly Parent, to commune in an intimate way with you. Suddenly, you feel his love surround you. You are filled with a wonderful warmth. You know it is his love. It is as though God had embraced you. God is speaking to the deepest inner part of your soul. Be quiet. Listen. God your heavenly Parent has something to say. If you heard him speak, or even if you only thought you heard him speak, write the words you heard in the space below.

What did God, your heavenly Parent say to you?

_____

_____

If you did not hear anything, don't be dismayed. This is an exercise that works well for some people; others may have difficulty imagining or experiencing it. You might like to choose one of the Scriptures from Psalms that seems to speak to your heart or need. Write the reference below as an indicator that God's personal words are already recorded in the Scriptures. We can hear him speak in an intimate way when we claim those Scriptures intimately.

Psalm _____ .

Tips for Parents (Optional)

(Leaders: *Begin the cassette* at previous stop to hear segment of human parenting.)

1/Once you have experienced the intimate, in-depth communication of God, you want to use that as a reminder in your human parenting. Hear your children tell you about their day. Do for them what your heavenly Parent does for you in listening to their intimate communication.

5

You Look Like Your Dad

Respecting our heavenly Father's discipline results in our becoming holy like him.

*A*T SOME POINT IN OUR JOURNEY to maturity, many of us make the vow that "we will never be like our parents." This does not mean we don't love them, but it is part of the natural process of individuation. One of life's great surprises, however, is that we can't escape the influence of our parents, no matter how much we try!

Test Yourself

The following fill-in-the-blank sentences are brief reminders of common expressions we hear people say to us (or some we even say to ourselves!).

1/You look just like _____!

2/I often find myself using the words and tone of voice _____ would use!

3/You sound exactly like _____ .

4/What would _____ have done in the same circumstances?

It's uncanny how imprinted we are with our parents' personalities. One of the ways this imprinting happens is through the modes and style of discipline our parents used to correct us. Circle the description (or descriptions) below that most closely describes your parents' form of discipline:

1/Lax and indifferent

2/Firm, but sometimes harsh or inconsistent

3/Firm but loving

4/Overly strict

5/Moderate controls based on mutual respect

6/Abusive

7/Other _____

Debrief as a Group

Choose one incident from your childhood which typifies the style of your parents' discipline and share it with the group. Or you might want to remember a time when you felt unjustly disciplined, and share that. (This is one of the few times you will receive adult group sympathy!)

Scripture Search

[5]You have forgotten that word of encouragement that addresses you as sons: "My son, do not make light of the Lord's discipline, and do not lose heart when he rebukes you, [6]because the Lord disciplines those he loves, and he punishes everyone he accepts as a son." [7]Endure hardship as discipline; God is treating you as

sons. For what son is not disciplined by his father? ⁸If you are not disciplined (and everyone undergoes discipline), then you are illegitimate children and not true sons. ⁹Moreover, we have all had human fathers who disciplined us and we respected them for it. How much more should we submit to the Father of our spirits and live! ¹⁰Our fathers disciplined us for a little while as they thought best; but God disciplines us for our good, that we may share in his holiness. ¹¹No discipline seems pleasant at the time, but painful. Later on, however, it produces a harvest of righteousness and peace for those who have been trained by it (Heb. 12: 5–11). (If you are a woman you may want to substitute the word "daughter" for "son" as you read these verses.)

1/List the verses that include a form of the word *chasten:*

2/Identify and copy from this passage any synonyms for the word *chasten:*

3/According to the passage, what are the benefits of chastisement?

4/In God's dealings with man, there is a clear distinction between *punishment* as a means of administering fair retribution for misdeeds, and *discipline,* which is designed to promote the growth of the disciplined one. Which of the two approaches is the writer of Hebrews talking about?

5/What is one of the major ways our heavenly Parent conforms us to his own characteristics so that we begin to look like him?

More Group Work

Discuss these questions in your group:

Can you remember a time when you were disciplined for the benefit of the person who disciplined you? Or did someone ever administer discipline which they thought was best but which was really damaging? When friends of your children visit your home, and all the children transgress some rule of the family, whose child is most likely to receive the punishment? Why?

Play Audio Cassette (Optional)

(Leaders: *Cue cassette* to Day Five, "You Look Like Your Dad."

Stop cassette just after David says, "And I've found it as a rule of thumb in my own life that again and again, regardless of the source, I'm wise to pay attention to it . . . God, you discipline me in whatever way you want and I'm open to it.")

Listen to Your Heavenly Parent

In what area are you being disciplined or trained by your heavenly Father right now?

_____

What result is your heavenly Parent attempting to achieve in your life?

_____

Complete the prayer below so that it becomes an expression of your own desire:

My Father,

I know I need to be disciplined in the area of

_____

_____

Help me to understand when you discipline me

_____

_____

Through divine chastisement, implant your image in me so people will say, "You look just like your Dad."

Tips for Parents (Optional)

(Leaders: *Begin the cassette* at the previous stop to hear the final segment on tips for parents.)

1/Use all the opportunities that present themselves as a means of changing behavior, as a learning experience—not just as a time to mete out judgment to our children.

2/Our goal as parents is to bring about different behavior just as God uses our life experiences to make us more like him.

3/Memorize Hebrews 12:10–11.

6

Spiritual Sibling Squabbles

Family members in God's household must work on caring
for each other.

*A*SK A GROUP OF PARENTS to name the problems in the family that
bother them the most and invariably, a good number will mention
fights between their children, or sibling rivalries. Our childhood
position in the family (firstborn, middle, last) and our relationship
with our brothers and sisters influence our adult outlook more than
most of us realize.

Test Yourself

You have exactly two minutes. Your group leader will keep track of
the time. In the following space, write as many positive synonyms
for the word *family* as you can in the time alloted.

Debrief as a Group

Take a moment and think about sibling squabbles. Choose one of
the following three situations and then relate your thoughts about
it to the group.

1/You are a child again, alone with the other children in your
family. Describe the circumstance in which you and your sibling(s)
are most likely to tangle.

2/You are a parent and your offspring have discovered the circumstance in which *they* are most likely to tangle. What is that circumstance and what is your reaction to it? Have you discovered any
helpful solutions for your siblings who squabble?

3/You are an adult but you still have siblings. What irritant still
evokes tension between you even though you are all grown?

Scripture Search

Read the following Scriptures aloud, taking turns around your
group.

*May the God who gives endurance and encouragement give you
a spirit of unity among yourselves as you follow Christ Jesus*
(Rom. 15:5).

You are all sons of God through faith in Christ Jesus (Gal. 3:26).

*. . . But God has combined the members of the body and has
given greater honor to the parts that lacked it, so that there
should be no division in the body, but that its parts should have
equal concern for each other. If one part suffers, every part suffers
with it; if one part is honored, every part rejoices with it* (1 Cor.
12:24–26).

*Consequently, you are no longer foreigners and aliens, but fellow
citizens with God's people and members of God's household* (Eph.
2:19).

Instead, speaking the truth in love, we will in all things grow up into him who is the Head, that is, Christ. From him the whole body, joined and held together by every supporting ligament, grows and builds itself up in love, as each part does its work (Eph. 4:15–16).

Pretend that these Scripture portions are each a chapter in an ancient book titled *The Family of God*. Brainstorm with the group some possible chapter titles for each portion.

1 / *(Rom. 15:5) Sample: "Unity or Else"*

_____

2 / *(Gal. 3:26) Sample: "One Big Happy Family"*

_____

3 / *(1 Cor. 12:24–26) Sample: "One for All and All for One"*

_____

4 / *(Eph. 2:19) Sample: "Naturalized Immigrants"*

_____

5 / *(Eph. 4:15–16) Sample: "Call on the Holy Osteopath"*

_____

Do these Scriptures reflect any of the positive synonyms you jotted down in the *Test Yourself* section?

Glance back over these Scripture passages and choose a word to describe how you feel about being part of the household of faith as it is presented in these verses.

_____

Share the word you have chosen with the group.

Now choose another word to describe how God must feel when he sees sibling squabbles in his family.

_____

Share this word with the group.

Play the Audio Cassette (Optional)

(Leaders: *Cue cassette* to Day Six, "Spiritual Sibling Squabbles."

Stop cassette at the end of the dialogue (entire message).)

Listen to Your Heavenly Parent

The group leader will time you again. Take one minute to write out words that describe the local church where you are now a family member.

_____

_____

How do you feel about being a part of this particular membership? Finish the following sentence: Examining my heart as honestly as possible, these are the feelings I have toward the local church where I belong:

_____

_____

In the continued quiet, ask yourself, "Am I having any sibling differences with *any* members of God's family? Is there a child of God whom I deliberately avoid? Is there one toward whom I harbor hateful feelings? Is there one to whom I have closed my heart and toward whom I feel a coldness?" Listen very carefully. Your heavenly Parent may use this silence to speak a name or two. Write what you are hearing.

_____

_____

Are there any cures found in the preceding Scriptures that might be administered to bring about Christian family unity? Look the verses over once more.

_____

_____

Do any of these remedies apply to the names you heard God speak to your heart? Write out one thing you can do to show your spiritual siblings that you want to really care for them.

_____

_____

More Group Work

How would you feel if you were a parent whose warring children put aside their jealousies and misunderstandings and began to listen and feel for each other, to forgive each other, becoming reconciled and working to repair broken relationships? In one sentence, write down what you think the heavenly Parent must feel when he sees this same dynamic begin to happen within his household of faith.

_____

_____

Share this sentence with the group. End this week's study with prayer that the actions and intents of his children in this group may bring pleasure to his Father-heart.

Tips for Parents (Optional)

(Ideas for these tips are presented in the body of the broadcast rather than at the end as in the other chapters.)

1/The family should provide a "belonging place" in which members may flesh out their Christianity.

2/Family members must work on caring for each other.

7

Pulling Your Own Weight

God insists that his offspring carry their fair share of family responsibilities.

*I*N THE STUDY OF CHILD DEVELOPMENT there is a concept known as the "developmental task," a learning level which generally follows upon the heels of another and which, if neglected, may prevent further developmental levels of learning. For instance, a child generally learns to read between kindergarten and third grade. A shift takes place around the fourth grade and from this point on, the child "reads to learn." If the developmental shift does not occur, learning in future grades may be stymied. Child experts emphasize that the process of building new developmental tasks upon earlier ones is essential to healthy maturation.

Test Yourself

The physical world often mirrors truths in the spiritual world. Spring returning again and again after winter is a picture of resurrection after death. Just as "developmental tasks" exist in the physical maturation of a child, "developmental tasks" also exist in the spiritual progress of the child of God. Take a few minutes to consider your own past spiritual journey.

1/Can you identify any kind of developmental process?

2/Were there some spiritual tasks you could not have accomplished had others not have been completed first? Write a few notes to remind yourself of this process in the following space.

_____

_____

_____

Debrief as a Group

Every family, even the most disorganized, maintains some kinds of rules for living together. Try to remember one rule that was important in your childhood family. Write it down and be prepared to share it with the group.

_____

Now think back to the jobs assigned to you as a child. Which one did you hate the most?

_____

What perspective do you hold about this job now that you are an adult?

_____

Scripture Search

The refrigerator door is a common spot for families to post messages and job lists. Let's pretend the heavenly Parent has just clipped a responsibility chart to your refrigerator door. Read over the following Scripture passage and list in the right-hand column the sorts of jobs God indicates he needs done in his family.

Romans 12	Responsibility
4Just as each of us has one body with many members, and these members do not all have the same function, 5so in Christ we who are many form one body, and each member belongs to all the others. 6We have different gifts, according to the grace given us. If a man's gift is prophesying, let him use it in proportion to his faith. 7If it is serving, let him serve; if it is teaching, let him teach; 8if it is encouraging, let him encourage; if it is contributing to the needs of others, let him give generously; if it is leadership, let him govern diligently; if it is showing mercy, let him do it cheerfully. 9Love must be sincere. Hate what is evil; cling to what is good. 10Be devoted to one another in brotherly love. Honor one another above yourselves. 11Never be lacking in zeal, but keep your spiritual fervor, serving the Lord. 12Be joyful in hope, patient in affliction, faithful in prayer. 13Share with God's people who are in need. Practice hospitality.	

Romans 12	Responsibility
[14]*Bless those who persecute you; bless and do not curse.* [15]*Rejoice with those who rejoice; mourn with those who mourn.* [16]*Live in harmony with one another. Do not be proud, but be willing to associate with people of low position. Do not be conceited.* [17]*Do not repay anyone evil for evil. Be careful to do what is right in the eyes of everybody.* [18]*If it is possible, as far as it depends on you, live at peace with everyone.* [19]*Do not take revenge, my friends, but leave room for God's wrath, for it is written: "It is mine to avenge; I will repay," says the Lord.* [20]*On the contrary: "If your enemy is hungry, feed him; if he is thirsty, give him something to drink. In doing this, you will heap burning coals on his head."*	

If you look carefully, you will find some basic household rules for the family of God included in this passage. See how many the group can pick out. But paraphrase them—put them in the modern idiom of today's family. For instance:

Basic Household Rules for Relationships in the Family of God

verse 6	In a family each member should pull his own weight!

(ruled table / blank lines)

Play the Audio Cassette (Optional)

(Leaders: *Cue cassette* to Day Seven, "Picking Up After Ourselves."

Stop Cassette just after David Mains says, ". . . when we talk about carrying a load, we are talking about a fair share; unto whom much is given—whether that be health or skills—much is required. So it's a person picking up that's important.")

Listen to Your Heavenly Parent

Every family seems to have one proverbial mess-maker. This is the member who always leaves disorder behind him/her and picks up after himself/herself only under intense persuasion. Or there are the perfectionists who insist on doing everything just right, preventing others from developing their own job performance skills. (Parents who always pick up after their children fall into this category.) Some contribute as little as possible and others simply can't get on with it—they seem to be stuck at a certain developmental level and consequently, progressive learning can't proceed. God's household has these kinds of family members as well.

1/Ask yourself, "What kind of responsibility do I take in God's household? Do I fit in one of the above categories?" If so, which one?

2/Look back over the Scripture portion from Romans 12. Most people discover they have both strong and weak points. Write below some of the areas where you have ability. Then intitial those areas on the Scripture page where you are weak. Be prepared to share one of each with the group. Strong points:

_____

_____

3/Fill in the following blanks as a means of contracting between yourself and your heavenly Parent to improve in one of your weak areas of job responsibility.

Dear Heavenly Father,
After examining Scripture, I realize I am weak in the area of

_____ . I suspect I don't

function well in this area because _____

_____ .

Help me to improve in pulling my own weight. One thing I can

do to grow up in this area is _____

_____ .

Thank you for being such an understanding Father.

More Group Work

As honestly as you are able, share with the group one of your strong areas and one area that needs improvement. The study time will end with each member praying for the person on his or her right. You might want to jot down what that person shares so you can remember how to pray.

Take time now to share, then end with prayer that goes around the room as each person prays for the person to his/her right.

Tips for Parents (Optional)

(Leaders: *Begin the cassette* at the previous stop to hear the final segment on tips for parents.)

1/To let children in our own family get by without doing a fair share of the household tasks is to do them a disservice.

2/It is equally important to teach them to be active participants in the household of God. Help your children to find areas in the church where they can serve.

8

Who Do You Love the Most?

Understanding God's individualized parenting releases his children from sibling comparisons.

*P*ARENTS WHO ATTEMPT TO TREAT their children with perfect equality often err as much in their child-raising as those who are guilty of gross favoritism. Each child is a unique individual in need of individualized attention. What is good for one may be all wrong for another. The wise parent attempts to understand each offspring in this individual fashion and adapts both discipline and nurture to what is best for the personality of each child.

The best-intentioned human parents often fail, but God, who is wholly loving, genuinely wise, completely fair, is the Parent we all long for. His individualized attention uniquely nurtures each of us, his children, when we are born into his family.

Debrief as a Group

Think of a situation where you felt you were definitely on the short end of someone's favoritism. List below the feelings this experience evoked in you. Discuss the incident with the group and your response to it.

Scripture Search

Partiality is one of the huge problems many people must cope with. Children often feel that parents or grandparents love another sibling more than themselves. Teens feel excluded from "the in-group." Workers on the job sense unequal distribution of favors or promotion from the boss. Read the following Scripture and see if you can conjecture what might have been behind Peter's question to Christ.

[15]When they had finished eating, Jesus said to Simon Peter, "Simon son of John, do you truly love me more than these?" "Yes, Lord," he said, "you know that I love you." Jesus said, "Feed my lambs." [16]Again Jesus said, "Simon son of John, do you truly love me?" He answered, "Yes, Lord, you know that I love you." Jesus said, "Take care of my sheep." [17]The third time he said to him, "Simon son of John, do you love me?" Peter was hurt because Jesus asked him the third time, "Do you love me?" He said, "Lord, you know all things; you know that I love you." Jesus said, "Feed my sheep. [18]I tell you the truth, when you were younger you dressed yourself and went where you wanted; but when you are old you will stretch out your hands, and someone else will dress you and lead you where you do not want to go." [19]Jesus said this to indicate the kind of death by which Peter would glorify God. Then he said to him, "Follow me!" [20]Peter turned and saw that the disciple whom Jesus loved was following them. (This was the one who had leaned back against Jesus at the supper and had said, "Lord, who is going to betray you?")

²¹*When Peter saw him, he asked, "Lord, what about him?"* ²²*Jesus answered, "If I want him to remain alive until I return, what is that to you? You must follow me."* ²³*Because of this, the rumor spread among the brothers that this disciple would not die. But Jesus did not say that he would not die; he only said, "If I want him to remain alive until I return, what is that to you?"* (John 21:15–23).

Scripture study is enhanced when we know as much as possible about the circumstances under which portions were written. Discuss the following questions:

1/What was the context in which this incident took place?

_____

2/Why did Christ ask his question three times?

_____

3/Why was Peter grieved?

_____

4/Who else may have heard this exchange between Peter and Christ?

_____

5/If one sign of good parenting is individualized child-rearing techniques, in what ways did Christ individualize his approach to fit the unique personality of the apostle Peter?

_____

6/Why do you think Peter attempted to turn Christ's attention to John? What are some of the reasons we as God's children ask, "What about that one?" or "Why do you love this one more than you love me?"

Test Yourself

Not only do we sometimes feel that our parents, friends, or close associates prefer someone else to ourselves, we often feel that God our Father plays favorites.

1/Have you ever experienced any negative feelings toward your heavenly Parent regarding what you feel might be his favoritism? If so, what has caused this feeling?

2/How do you know when someone loves you?

3/Each of us, because of our background and unique personality, has an individual economy by which we measure love. We call it the love exchange, the measurement by which individual people give, receive, and understand love. For instance, one person's love exchange may be measured in terms of thoughtful, spontaneous gifts. Another person's love exchange may be measured in terms of carefully remembered anniversaries and special days. Our human alienation is often caused because we do not understand and therefore, misinterpret how people close to us measure love. Write below the particular and personal exchange that expresses love to you.

4/How do you measure the love exchange of your heavenly Parent? If God individualized his parenting to fit your particular personality and needs, by what means would you know that he loved and cared for you?

_____

_____

_____

5/Finish the following sentence: Lord, I often have problems experiencing your love; I need to know you love me by

_____

_____

Play the Audio Cassette (Optional)

(Leaders: *Cue cassette* to Day Eight, "Who Do You Love the Most?"

Stop cassette after Karen Mains says, "When I run I feel his pleasure, and I think that when we feel the intimate pleasure of God, it doesn't matter how he chooses to work with our brothers and sisters.")

Listen to Your Heavenly Parent

God supernaturally individualizes his attention to all his children. Often we can't hear him speak about his individualized love to us because we don't set aside enough time for quiet in which to listen to him.

1/Be still now for a few moments before this study session ends. What words or actions from your heavenly Parent would assure you of his individual favor?

_____

_____

_____

2/Answer the question: How do I bring my heavenly Parent pleasure?

_____

Tips for Parents (Optional)

(Leaders: *Begin the cassette* at the previous stop to hear the final segment on tips for parents.)

1/Do not compare your children. Enjoy each one.

2/Constantly re-affirm your love.

3/Individualize your attention to your children's needs.

9

How Shall We Behave?

To know how to behave properly, spiritual children must closely observe the perfect role model of their heavenly Father.

WHO THREW AWAY THE ETIQUETTE BOOK? Thirty years ago, social rules were far more clearly defined than they are today. In some ways, this has produced a social relaxation that is healthy; but in other ways, it has produced confusion—we often don't know how to behave in social situations.

Debrief as a Group

Did you have an etiquette book on your childhood family bookshelf? Recall and describe some of the rules that existed when you were growing up and that are no longer considered important.

Discuss the question: What social negatives result from the fact that the etiquette book has been discarded?

Test Yourself

1/Think of one lesson you learned as a child regarding how you were supposed to behave toward other people.

_____

_____

2/How did you learn this lesson?
through formal teaching   out of a book   through example
by a specific phrase repeated over and over by parents or a teacher

3/As you reflect, which do you remember more—what your parents said to you or how they behaved toward you?

_____

_____

4/Did anyone in authority over you ever set up a false behavior standard, in effect, "Do what I say, but don't do what I do?" Write it down.

_____

5/How did you respond?

_____

6/As a child, how were you disappointed by hypocrisy discovered in the life of someone you admired?

_____

7/Experts tell us that nearly 90% of the lessons (both positive and negative) that we learn in childhood are absorbed through the behavior modeled by an adult or older peer. Identify those special people who were role models for you. Write down their names in the first column and the ways that they influenced you in the second column.

Role models	Influences

Play the Audio Cassette (Optional)

(Leaders: *Cue cassette* to Day Nine, "How Shall We Behave?"

Stop cassette just after Karen Mains says, ". . . we have become convinced in our own parenting as we see other children when they become adults say, 'I learned this from my parents . . . when they acted in such a way' . . . so I think this is a wonderful application for our generation that is confused in its behavior.")

Scripture Search

Read the following Scripture out loud. This is the last half of Romans 12. (The first half was studied in Week Seven.)

⁹Love must be sincere. Hate what is evil; cling to what is good. ¹⁰Be devoted to one another in brotherly love. Honor one another above yourselves. ¹¹Never be lacking in zeal, but keep your spiritual fervor, serving the Lord. ¹²Be joyful in hope, patient in affliction, faithful in prayer. ¹³Share with God's people who are in need. Practice hospitality.

¹⁴Bless those who persecute you; bless and do not curse. ¹⁵Rejoice with those who rejoice; mourn with those who mourn. ¹⁶Live in harmony with one another. Do not be proud, but be willing to associate with people of low position. Do not be conceited.

¹⁷Do not repay anyone evil for evil. Be careful to do what is right in the eyes of everybody. ¹⁸If it is possible, as far as it depends on you, live at peace with everyone. ¹⁹Do not take revenge, my friends, but leave room for God's wrath, for it is written: "It is mine to avenge; I will repay," says the Lord. ²⁰On the contrary:

> *"If your enemy is hungry, feed him;*
> *if he is thirsty, give him something to drink.*
> *In doing this, you will heap burning coals on his head."*

²¹Do not be overcome by evil, but overcome evil with good (Romans 12:9–21).

1/In a sense, the Scriptures are God's etiquette book which reveal how the heavenly Parent expects his children to behave. Take the Romans passage and divide these "rules of etiquette" into attitude behavior and action behavior. You can write out the verse references if you prefer but your learning process will be enhanced if you write out phrases.

Attitude Behavior	Action Behavior

2/Some rules given prohibit certain behaviors. List what you should *not* do.

_____

_____

_____

3/Discuss the following questions:
Why are these rules of behavior so different from the etiquette standards of society? Why are they so often ignored by the children in the household of faith? What is a practical plan for beginning to live by these principles? (In other words, how do we turn these ideas into actions in our own lives?)

Now look at this passage from 1 Peter.

²¹To this you were called, because Christ suffered for you, leaving you an example, that you should follow in his steps.

> *²²"He committed no sin,*
> *and no deceit was found in his mouth."*

²³When they hurled their insults at him, he did not retaliate; when he suffered, he made no threats. Instead, he entrusted himself to him who judges justly. ²⁴He himself bore our sins in his body on the tree, so that we might die to sins and live for righteousness; by his wounds you have been healed. ²⁵For you were like sheep going astray, but now you have returned to the Shepherd and Overseer of your souls (1 Peter 2:21–25).

4/Discuss the following questions:
In what ways did Christ become a role model for us? What bearing does this passage have on the question, "How shall we behave?" When we have such a compelling model, why do we so often behave in ways we know are inappropriate?

Listen to Your Heavenly Parent

1/In the quiet, look over the Scriptures from Romans 12 again. Listen to your own thoughts, and to the quiet voice of the Holy Spirit within. Is something being whispered regarding your behavior? Write down what you are thinking and hearing.

_____

_____

_____

2/Most newspapers carry advice columns that answer the questions of people who do not know how to handle their problems. Write a Dear Abba (Papa) letter.
Dear Abba,
I am puzzled as to how to behave in this area of life:

_____

_____

_____

Help me to understand how you would behave in the same circumstances. From what I know of your nature I think that:

_____

Tips for Parents (Optional)

(Leaders: *Begin the cassette* at the previous stop to hear the final segment on tips for parents.)

1/Stress the concept of showing who God is.

2/Our relationship with earthly parents will affect our relationship with our heavenly Parent.

10

New Beginnings

Sons and daughters who fail come to their senses when
they realize that God wants to help them begin again.

*O*NE OF THE MOST REMARKABLE QUALITIES about the nature of God
is that he is a redemptive God who offers opportunities to his
children to begin over again, and again, and again. He is the God of
resurrections, large and small, in our lives. He is the one who
creates and re-creates, who uses even the mistakes in our lives
constructively when we let him. He is the one who even turns our
rebellion into usefulness.

Test Yourself

1/Identify any area in your life you have always wished you could
live over again, do better at this time, have a second chance at.

2/Think of one time in your life when you *were* given another chance to start over again.

_____

3/Name one particularly difficult developmental skill that you have successfully accomplished.

_____

Scripture Search

As a group, name some of the new beginnings that God has built into our lives which may be frequently overlooked.

_____

_____

Now take turns reading the following Scripture (or appoint a good reader to read this dramatic story aloud).

[11]Jesus continued: There was a man who had two sons. [12]The younger one said to his father, "Father, give me my share of the estate." So he divided his property between them. [13]Not long after that, the younger son got together all he had, set off for a distant country and there squandered his wealth in wild living. [14]After he had spent everything, there was a severe famine in that whole country, and he began to be in need. [15]So he went and hired himself out to a citizen of that country, who sent him to his fields to feed pigs. [16]He longed to fill his stomach with the pods that the pigs were eating, but no one gave him anything. [17]When he came to his senses, he said, "How many of my father's hired men have food to spare, and here I am starving to death! [18]I will set out and go back to my father and say to him: Father, I have sinned against heaven and against you. [19]I am no longer worthy to be called your son; make me like one of your hired men." [20]So he got up and went to his father. But while he was still a long

way off, his father saw him and was filled with compassion for him; he ran to his son, threw his arms around him and kissed him. ²¹The son said to him, "Father, I have sinned against heaven and against you. I am no longer worthy to be called your son." ²²But the father said to his servants, "Quick! Bring the best robe and put it on him. Put a ring on his finger and sandals on his feet. ²³Bring the fattened calf and kill it. Let's have a feast and celebrate. ²⁴For this son of mine was dead and is alive again; he was lost and is found." So they began to celebrate. ²⁵Meanwhile, the older son was in the field. When he came near the house, he heard music and dancing. ²⁶So he called one of the servants and asked him what was going on. ²⁷"Your brother has come," he replied, "and your father has killed the fattened calf because he has him back safe and sound." ²⁸The older brother became angry and refused to go in. So his father went out and pleaded with him. ²⁹But he answered his father, "Look! All these years I've been slaving for you and never disobeyed your orders. Yet you never gave me even a young goat so I could celebrate with my friends. ³⁰But when this son of yours who has squandered your property with prostitutes comes home, you kill the fattened calf for him!" ³¹"My son," the father said, "you are always with me, and everything I have is yours. ³²But we had to celebrate and be glad, because this brother of yours was dead and is alive again; he was lost and is found" (Luke 15:11–32).

1/Even though this portion of Scripture is one of the most frequently-studied when Christians address the nature of God the Father, its tremendous implications for each of us never grow stale. Write down the personality characteristics of the main characters in this tale. Describe the personality of:

The Prodigal Son

_____

The Older Brother

_____

The Father

_____

2/Draw some conclusions regarding this father's method of discipline. Why did he give his son his inheritance when he probably knew the boy would be a spendthrift with it?

_____

_____

_____

3/When the prodigal returned, utterly disillusioned, what things did the father *not* say to him that he could have said?

_____

_____

_____

4/What might your parents have said to you if you had been the prodigal returning home after a life of dissipation? Think a moment, write this out, then share your answer with the group.

_____

_____

_____

5/This parable is obviously about a loving, forgiving Parent who believes in giving his children an opportunity to begin again. Each of us has an area of failure in our life where we would like to turn a new leaf. Where would *you* like a new beginning? Feel free either to share with the group or not.

_____

_____

_____

6/This Scripture gives us clues as to how to begin anew. List below the steps the prodigal took to return home so he could start fresh.

_____

_____

Play the Audio Cassette (Optional)

(Leaders: *Cue cassette* to Day Ten, "New Beginnings."

Stop cassette just after David Mains says, ". . . this day now help me, and as I come through this day, I'll be ready for tomorrow and I'll pray a 'this day' prayer then.")

Listen to Your Heavenly Parent

1/Use the quiet to fill in the blanks in the following prayer. This form will serve as a guided monologue between you and your heavenly Parent.

Oh, Father,

I have failed _____.

I want a new beginning _____.

I confess _____.

I need to _____.

The part that will be hard for me is _____

_____ .

I need to hear you say _____

_____ .

One of the reasons we don't take advantage of the new beginnings that God offers us is that we allow ourselves to be overwhelmed by the effort of beginning again. Groups that help alcoholics and smokers overcome their addictions insist that these people develop a one-day-at-a-time mentality. We must all learn not to look back at the enormity of our mistakes, particularly when God has forgiven us and when we have received that forgiveness; but we must also learn not to look ahead at the mountains that need to be climbed.

2/In a sense, all of us must learn to live one day at a time. We must learn to live this day, each single new day, well. Compose a "this day" prayer regarding the area of beginning again that is most personal to you. Write the prayer below.

Dear Lord,

This day, I _____

_____

_____

_____

_____

_____

_____

Amen.

Tips for Parents (Optional)

(Leaders: *Begin the cassette* at the previous stop to hear the final segment on tips for parents.)

1/Encourage children to begin over, start over. Say, "I'll help you. It's okay. You can try again."

2/Love them regardless of what they do. Let them be confident of that love.

11

Reading of the Greatest Will

The provision of a heavenly Parent's magnificent
inheritance enables his heirs to live with an eternal
perspective.

*N*O NOTIFICATION IS AS INTRIGUING as the one which informs us that
we have been included in someone's will. Just as earthly parents
attempt to provide after their own deaths for the children whom
they love, so our heavenly Parent has promised a fabulous inheritance of accumulated riches for us *after our death.*

Debrief as a Group

Has anyone in the group ever received an inheritance? Or has
anyone been present at the reading of a will? Share when and how
this happened, then read the following notification:

> Good news! You are the recipient of an inheritance from a distant
> and aged relative who died several years ago. The estate has just
> been settled. You have inherited $10,000. The stipulation in the
> will states that you cannot bank or invest this money.

Brainstorm with the group how you are going to spend this windfall.

_____

_____

Scripture Search

Scripture also tells us that our heavenly Parent has provided us with a magnificent inheritance. Read these verses aloud:

So you are no longer a slave, but a son; and since you are a son, God has made you also an heir (Gal. 4:7).

Now if we are children, then we are heirs—heirs of God and co-heirs with Christ, if indeed we share in his sufferings in order that we may also share in his glory (Rom. 8:17).

³Praise be to the God and Father of our Lord Jesus Christ! In his great mercy he has given us new birth into a living hope through the resurrection of Jesus Christ from the dead, ⁴and into an inheritance that can never perish, spoil or fade—kept in heaven for you, ⁵who through faith are shielded by God's power until the coming of the salvation that is ready to be revealed in the last time. ⁶In this you greatly rejoice, though now for a little while you may have had to suffer grief in all kinds of trials. ⁷These have come so that your faith—of greater worth than gold, which perishes even though refined by fire—may be proved genuine and may result in praise, glory and honor when Jesus Christ is revealed. ⁸Though you have not seen him, you love him; and even though you do not see him now, you believe in him and are filled with an inexpressible and glorious joy, ⁹for you are receiving the goal of your faith, the salvation of your souls (1 Peter 1:3–9).

Discuss the Following Questions:

1/What is an heir or an heiress?

2/What is the nature of the Christian's inheritance?

3/If you know that a substantial amount of money has been provided for you in your parents' will, how does that make you feel regarding the future?

4/What should the inheritance your heavenly Parent has provided for you make you feel regarding your spiritual future?

5/Knowing you have a magnificent spiritual inheritance should alter the way you live your life now. Brainstorm some differences this knowledge should make in present lifestyles. What does this magnificent spiritual inheritance reveal about the nature of your heavenly Parent?

Test Yourself

Circle the answer that best describes your response to the statements below.

1/I think about my heavenly inheritance
a/frequently
b/once in awhile
c/never think about it

2/I am probably more concerned about earthly inheritances than I am about heavenly inheritances.
a/That's where I am
b/This is a new idea to me
c/Increasingly I am anticipating a more spiritual inheritance

3/The fact of a heavenly inheritance has no emotional impact on my life.
a/Good description
b/It has some emotional impact
c/Actually, it means a great deal to me

4/When I think of a heavenly inheritance, all I can think of are crowns and streets of gold and this has no reality in terms of my everyday world.
a/I feel that way
b/I see those words as symbols for even more meaningful realities
c/What's wrong with crowns and streets of gold?

5/I am consciously readjusting my daily living in terms of what I understand about my future inheritance.
a/Oh boy, I've got some work to do
b/This has had some influence on me although I admit it hasn't been major
c/I think continually in terms of the future's bearing on my every-day living
d/As I get older it has more and more influence

Play the Audio Cassette (Optional)

(Leaders: *Cue cassette* to Day Eleven, "Reading of the Greatest Will."

Stop cassette at end of message.)

More Group Work

Listen. A will is being read. Choose someone to read 1 Peter 1:3–6 (below) and insert his/her name in the blanks.

Praise be to God and the Father of our Lord Jesus Christ! In his

great mercy he has given _____ new birth into a
living hope through the resurrection of Jesus Christ from the dead,
and into an inheritance that can never perish, spoil or fade—kept in

heaven for _____ , who through faith are shield-
ed by God's power until the coming of the salvation that is ready to

be revealed in the last time. In this _____ greatly

rejoice(s), though now for a little while _____
may have to suffer grief in all kinds of trials.

Listen to Your Heavenly Parent

Each person needs to personalize Scripture so that it takes an
individual hold in his/her private life. Personalize Galatians 4:7 and
Romans 8:17.

So you, _____ are no more a slave, but a

_____ , and since you are a _____

_____ , then God has made you, _____ ,
also an heir.

Now if we are children, then you, _____ , are an

_____ of God and _____

with Christ; if indeed _____ shares in his suffer-

ings in order that _____ may also share in his
glory.

If an aged and distant relative left you an inheritance of $10,000 to
spend at your discretion, your feelings would probably be those of

overwhelming surprise and gratitude. Your heavenly Father is preparing for you an immeasurable inheritance. Write a prayer of gratitude, or a psalm of praise, expressing to him how you feel about his loving largesse:

Lord,
I am surprised at how wealthy you really are!

_____

_____

_____

_____

_____

_____

Amen

Tips for Parents

(Not included as a separate part of this message.)

12

Being Children Again

Unlike earthly parents, our heavenly Father measures our spiritual maturity by the amount of dependence we choose to place on him.

*G*OD IS THE PERFECT PARENT and when we look at his example we can draw lessons, if we are parents ourselves, as to how to raise our own children. In the matter of dependence and independence, however, we cannot do what God does. Wise earthly parents raise their offspring to become independent, whole, self-sufficient adults. Conversely, God raises his children to become increasingly dependent upon him, and this unique relationship is one of the great struggles of the Christian journey.

Debrief as a Group

The healthy emotional and psychological process of separation from one's parents is called individuation. What are some of the ways we can identify healthy adult independence?

What does it look like? What does it not look like? How can we achieve it for ourselves? How can we help our children (if we have children) achieve it?

Scripture Search

Whereas maturity on the human level is measured by healthy independence, maturity on the spiritual level is measured by dependence. Have group members read the following verses aloud:

My children, I will be with you only a little longer. You will look for me, and just as I told the Jews, so I tell you now: Where I am going, you cannot come (John 13:33).

How great is the love the Father has lavished on us, that we should be called children of God! And that is what we are! The reason the world does not know us is that it did not know him (1 John 3:1).

For you did not receive a spirit that makes you a slave again to fear, but you received the Spirit of sonship. And by him we cry, "Abba, Father." The Spirit himself testifies with our spirit that we are God's children (Romans 8:15–16).

These Scriptures make it abundantly clear that we are to consider ourselves children of God. Discuss with the group, however, your ideas about childlikeness and childishness and how they are different. Is there such a thing as an unhealthy dependence on our heavenly Parent? Why, or why not?

_____

_____

_____

The following passage gives us guidelines on how to develop child-likeness, a healthy dependency upon God, our heavenly Parent. Ask someone to read the passage aloud.

¹I am the true vine and my Father is the gardener. ²He cuts off every branch in me that bears no fruit, while every branch that does bear fruit he trims clean so that it will be even more fruitful. ³You are already clean because of the word I have spoken to you. ⁴Remain in me, and I will remain in you. No branch can bear fruit by itself; it must remain in the vine. Neither can you bear fruit unless you remain in me. ⁵I am the vine; you are the branches. If a man remains in me and I in him, he will bear much fruit; apart from me you can do nothing. ⁶If anyone does not remain in me, he is like a branch that is thrown away and withers; such branches are picked up, thrown into the fire and burned. ⁷If you remain in me and my words remain in you, ask whatever you wish, and it will be given you. ⁸This is to my Father's glory, that you bear much fruit, showing yourselves to be my disciples. ⁹As the Father has loved me, so have I loved you. Now remain in my love. ¹⁰If you obey my commands, you will remain in my love, just as I have obeyed my Father's commands and remain in his love. ¹¹I have told you this so that my joy may be in you and that your joy may be complete (John 15:1–11).

Discuss the following questions. According to this passage:

1/What are the results of abiding in Christ?

_____

_____

2/What are the results of not abiding in Christ?

_____

_____

3/As a study group, attempt to define the word *abide*. Can the word *depend* be adequately substituted for the word *abide* in this passage? What other shades of meaning does the word *abide* hold?

_____

_____

_____

4/What is the relationship of the Father to the children who abide in the vine?

_____

5/Why do you think Christ chose the vine as a symbol to define his disciples' relationship to him?

_____

_____

6/Brainstorm the ways a mature relationship with our heavenly Parent is different from a mature relationship with our earthly parents.

_____

_____

_____

Test Yourself

1/Who are the people you depend on when you need counsel or wisdom?

_____

2/Who are the people you go to when you need help in physical/ emotional emergencies or crises?

_____

3/When do you consider (if ever) that you have a heavenly Parent who is eager to help you with counsel, wisdom, and material aid?

_____

4/When you need help, who do you think of, phone, go to *first?*

_____

Play the Audio Cassette (Optional)

(Leaders: *Cue cassette* to Day Twelve, "Being Children Again."

Stop cassette just after David Mains says, ". . . this is the idea that we find in Scripture from our heavenly Father as well . . . Now, how do you like that?")

Listen to Your Heavenly Parent

The Romans 8:15–16 passage suggests such an intimate relationship with our heavenly Father that we address him with childhood endearment. *Abba* can be translated "Papa" or "Daddy." Lay aside your adult pretensions and in your mind become a little child again. Sit close to your heavenly Parent (some of you may even want to crawl into his lap). Take his hand and cry, *Abba*. Finish the following prayer.

Dear Papa.

I need to learn _____ .

In moments of need, help me to learn to come to you first. There is one area I need to talk to you about right now.

_____

_____

Amen.

More Group Work

You have been together for twelve sessions studying the characteristic of God's nature summed up in the word *Parent.* Take a few moments at the end of this week's study and share one special lesson you have learned and have been able to integrate into your personal life.

Tips for Parents (Optional)

(Leaders: *Begin the cassette* at the previous stop to hear the final segment on tips for parents.)

As you raise your children, work not only to help them become independent of you, but to become more dependent on God. Hand them over to him.

WEEKLY LEADER'S NOTES

Each study includes five basic sections: TEST YOURSELF, DE-BRIEF AS A GROUP, PLAY THE AUDIO CASSETTE (optional), SCRIPTURE SEARCH, and LISTEN TO YOUR HEAVENLY PARENT. Though they are arranged in different order from week to week, these sections are the basic format for each study.

Because of the nature of this study, it is important to emphasize as soon as possible that *confidences can be shared in a group when confidentiality is promised.* Honesty and trust are proportionate to the measure of the confidentiality maintained. From time to time during the study you may have to remind the group that confidentiality is a priestly function of the body of Christ that each member, including yourself, must strive to maintain.

Study One—Daddy, Do You Love Me?

Key Truth: Christians, regardless of age, need to experience the security of God's strong parental love.
Goal: Through interaction with Scripture and each other, group

members will actually feel the assurance of the words of the heavenly Father, "I love you."

Comments: This is the first week of study. The different sections are designed to introduce the group to the content of the study but to also gain familiarity with each other. Make sure that the group actually participates in the time of quiet provided in the section, LISTEN TO YOUR HEAVENLY PARENT. It is during these moments that the Holy Spirit will have the opportunity to apply everything that has been learned and discussed.

Study Two—Who Am I?

Key Truth: Self-identity is discovered only in knowing the wonder of our heavenly parentage.

Goal: To introduce to the group the idea that theology, the study of God and his relationship to man and the world, must be an essential part of our learning process if we are to know who we are and how we are to function in the world.

Comments: This study may evoke some painful links with past childhood experiences. It will certainly assist members in examining their relationship with their own parents. Pray that God will give you unusual sensitivity and the ability to know when to prod more and when to cease from prodding.

Study Three—Our Heavenly Parent's Two Great Expectations

Key Truth: God's children function best as they obey his clear parental guidelines to love him and their neighbors.

Goal: To choose specific names and actions to improve the quality of love toward God and members of his family.

Comments: The inductive study in the SCRIPTURE SEARCH section employs an innovative approach. Make sure that you understand this technique before you attempt to lead the group in it.

Study Four—An In-Depth Relationship with God

Key Truth: God's children experience an in-depth relationship when they take advantage of their heavenly Father's intimate communication.

Goal: To begin to experience God's intimacy.

Comments: The purpose of the sentence completion test in the TEST YOURSELF section is to help the group make the connection between their feelings toward their own parents which have been transferred to their feelings about God. No discussion questions are listed in this section of the workbook, but you might introduce discussion by asking if anyone has any observations. This is left to your discretion.

Study Five—You Look Like Your Dad

Key Truth: Family members in God's household must work on caring for each other.

Goal: To discover the positive, loving aspect of God's discipline.

Comments: Listen carefully as people share how they were disciplined in their own childhood. Sometimes the most wretched of tales can be shared in the most matter-of-fact ways. Be very sensitive to wounds that may still exist. You might ask, "How did that make you feel as a child?" if you sense the question is needed, or you might ask, "How do you feel about that form of discipline now that you are an adult?"

Study Six—Spiritual Sibling Squabbles

Key Truth: Family members in God's household must work on caring for each other.

Goal: To feel God's own hurt when his children fight and damage each other.

Comments: Brainstorming titles in the SCRIPTURE SEARCH section may be a little hard for some. Sample titles have been included to get the idea across. You may want to think of one or two before the actual study, just to be ready to "prime the pump" if ideas are slow.

Study Seven—Pulling Your Own Weight

Key Truth: God insists that his offspring carry their fair share of family responsibility.

Goal: To examine one's relationship to work responsibilities in the family of God.

Comments: Depending on how comfortable the group is with one another by this time, you might ask them to read aloud the contract-prayer included in the LISTEN TO YOUR HEAVENLY PARENT section. Use your own discretion. Make sure group members pray for each other. This is a wonderful means of building Christian lives together.

Study Eight—Who Do You Love the Most?

Key Truth: Understanding God's individualized parenting releases his children from sibling comparisons.

Goal: To develop specific measurements by which you can know that God loves you uniquely, which will remove the need to compare yourself to his other children.

Comments: In the SCRIPTURE SEARCH section, the group is asked to discover the context in which this story was written. Make sure you are prepared with background material yourself before you head into this discussion. On your own, review ahead the chapters of John 21.

Study Nine—How Shall We Behave?

Key Truth: To know how to behave properly, spiritual children must closely observe the perfect role model of their heavenly Father.

Goal: To begin developing a pattern of closely observing God in order to discover what behavior is appropriate in our times.

Comments: Don't be tempted to hurry through the SCRIPTURE SEARCH section. This Romans passage is rich with behavioral principles. The longer you are able to dwell on it, the more the group will be able to discover.

Study Ten—New Beginnings

Key Truth: Sons and daughters who fail come to their senses when they realize that God wants to help them begin again.

Goal: To find courage and exercise discipline, because of God's character, to make new beginnings in specific areas.

Comments: When a group feels comfortable with each other, and has shared growth experiences together, the idea begins to develop that shortcomings can be told without fear of judgment. That is a form of confessing our sins one to another, which we are instructed to do in James. This week deals with forgiveness and confession in a non-directive fashion. Be aware of the need to give the group opportunity to share weaknesses as a process of clearing the way for new becomings.

Study Eleven—Reading of the Greatest Will

Key Truth: The provision of a heavenly Parent's magnificent inheritance enables his heirs to live with an eternal perspective.
Goal: To begin developing an eternal perspective on God's care that influences daily living.
Comments: The technique of personalizing Scripture by putting one's name in the passage has been used off and on during these weeks of study. Hearing one's name spoken aloud while it is inserted in the passage is often a powerful affirmation of truth. As time permits, have several (and perhaps even all) of the group members read aloud the passage in the LISTEN TO YOUR HEAVENLY PARENT section.

Study Twelve—Being Children Again

Key Truth: Unlike earthly parents, our heavenly Father measures our spiritual maturity by the amount of dependence we choose to place on him.
Goal: To identify one's unidentified areas of spiritual independence; then determine to become dependent upon God in that area.
Comments: This study ends with the section: MORE GROUP WORK in which the members are asked to share one lesson learned during the study which they have been able to integrate into their personal life. Make sure you have taken some time to discover an area of growth in your own life so that you will be able to share it, and if need be, start the sharing with it.